W9-ASZ-290

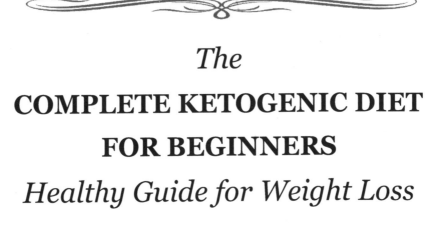

The

COMPLETE KETOGENIC DIET FOR BEGINNERS

Healthy Guide for Weight Loss

PETER BRAGG

Text Copyright © Peter Bragg

All rights reserved. No part of this guide may be reproduced in any form without permission in writing from the publisher except in the case of brief quotations embodied in critical articles or reviews.

Legal & Disclaimer

The information contained in this book and its contents is not designed to replace or take the place of any form of medical or professional advice; and is not meant to replace the need for independent medical, financial, legal or other professional advice or services, as may be required. The content and information in this book have been provided for educational and entertainment purposes only.

The content and information contained in this book have been compiled from sources deemed reliable, and it is accurate to the best of the Author's knowledge, information, and belief. However, the Author cannot guarantee its accuracy and validity and cannot be held liable for any errors and/or omissions. Further, changes are periodically made to this book as and when needed. Where appropriate and/or necessary, you must consult a professional (including but not limited to your doctor, attorney, financial advisor or such other professional advisor) before using any of the suggested remedies, techniques, or information in this book.

Upon using the contents and information contained in this book, you agree to hold harmless the Author from and against any damages, costs, and expenses, including any legal fees potentially resulting from the application of any of the information provided by this book. This disclaimer applies to any loss, damages or injury caused by the use and application, whether directly or indirectly, of any advice or information presented, whether for breach of contract, tort, negligence, personal injury, criminal intent, or under any other cause of action.

You agree to accept all risks of using the information presented in this book.

You agree that by continuing to read this book, where appropriate and/or necessary, you shall consult a professional (including but not limited to your doctor, attorney, or financial advisor or such other advisor as needed) before using any of the suggested remedies, techniques, or information in this book.

Table of Contents

Book Description

Perhaps it would be better to think of the ketogenic diet regarding a lifestyle rather than just another fad diet. This lifestyle does not rely on the use of your unrelenting willpower to lose weight and gain health benefits.

Instead, all it requires is that we gain a better understanding of what it is that we have been incorrectly doing for the last fifty years, and how the errors of our ways have to lead to an explosion of excess fat, obesity, and Type II Diabetes in our society.

For years we have been drip fed a constant barrage of misinformation that stated that the sudden dramatic increase in our body weight was all caused by overeating or exercising too little, implying the burden of guilt lay squarely on our shoulders. In fact, if you were able to show this lifestyle plan to your grandparents, there would be nothing there that would come as a surprise to them.

This system is going to take you back to an era before the food pyramid was so heavily promoted as the basis for our day to day eating habits; to a time that predates fast or industrially prepared food; to a time when almost the entire population was lean without having to count calories or sweat it out for hours down at the local gym.

Did you know that the United States currently has the highest obesity rates for both children and adults in the entire world? You could say that this is attributed to our lack of physical activity and our need to overeat when we do too little. However, I firmly believe that this is a result of the intake of too many carbohydrates. The body only utilizes what it needs, and the rest is stored as fat. I'm not saying that consuming too much protein or fats is right either, but realistically speaking, it's often harder to consume too much protein or fat because of their filling nature. Carbohydrates, on the other hand, are a beast altogether, exceptionally refined carbs. Most people eat bread, bagels, doughnuts, cakes, pancakes, waffles, and cookies for breakfast. For lunch, people often choose options like pasta, white rice, and French fries. Potatoes are a common side choice for dinner and maybe some chicken and vegetables. Most often desserts are also full of refined carbohydrates. Can you see where I am going with this? We are consuming too many carbs! If you want to lose weight, have increased energy levels and restore your health, reducing your carbohydrate intake is the solution.

So, what exactly *is* the Ketogenic Diet anyway? At its most basic level, the Ketogenic Diet is all about science (which is why so many people are enjoying its effectiveness!). By tapping into your body's natural food processing system, the Ketogenic Diet supports healthy digestion and converts your body's natural food storages into energy. The result? Faster weight loss, increased strength, and even mental clarity!

Introduction

This book is designed in a way that is easy to understand, about the secrets of the ketogenic diet, ketosis, and the countless health benefits associated with this lifestyle change.

Ketogenic diets have been used for thousands of years for their many health benefits, ease of implementation, and just because of the environments we evolved in.

Surprisingly, the Ketogenic diet was not created as a weight loss system. Instead, it was initially designed as an effective way to inhibit seizures in epileptic patients. It is intended to make sure the body gets enough protein and nutrients to stay healthy and energized, but not so many that it gains weight.

Over the years, as the diet gained in popularity, it began to be used for additional therapies, including the treatment of rare metabolic diseases, brain tumors, autism, depression, migraine headaches, and even Type 2 Diabetes. It has also been used for traumatic brain injuries, strokes, Parkinson's, and Alzheimer's disease. Oncologist even recommends this diet to cancer patients.

Because this diet works to improve health, while also decreasing weight, it has become a popular choice for everyone who wishes to lose weight, live a healthy lifestyle, or both. It is the best way to rapidly lose weight, without sacrificing your health or taking harmful drugs.

The Ketogenic diet is very scientific in how it works. It is designed to put the body in a state of ketosis. This state is reached when your body starts burning fat stores for fuel, instead of sugars. As you can imagine, burning the storage of fat is exactly what you need to do to lose the type of weight that you want to lose, while maintaining your muscles.

Along with burning fat stores, ketosis has a neurological effect that will leave you feeling happier and less hungry. Both of these results will further help you lose any amount of weight you want. Because it is a healthy way to eat, you can continue with the Ketogenic diet indefinitely to maintain the ideal weight for your body type.

At the completion of this book, you will have a much better understanding of the Keto diet and be able to experiment with the different recipes.

Benefits of Keto Diet

The list of health benefits secured from a Keto Diet will never be ending. Nevertheless, for your convenience, a few of the more significant health benefits that you can gain from a Keto Diet will be explained.

- **Epilepsy**: Since Ketogenic diet is a diet that features high fat, low carbohydrate, and controlled consumption of protein, it causes the body to use fat as the primary energy source energy. In a lot of epileptic cases, switching to a Ketogenic diet has resulted in a lowered incidence of seizures. Exercise care and supervision when children are following the diet.

- **Reversing Type 2 Diabetes**: This is one of the benefits of being on a Ketogenic diet. There are many success stories about this diet, which research has proven is a result of lowering the amount of carbohydrate that you consume, and as a result, your blood sugar level is brought to natural homeostasis. It is important to note that carb stimulates the body system to discharge the hormone called insulin. So, when carb intake is lowered, the body does not release more insulin to control the blood sugar which will, in turn, increase the burning of fat that has been stored in the body. How then does this work in reversing Type 2 diabetes? The answer to the question is simple. The fundamental problem faced by people with diabetes is a high amount of blood sugar that comes primarily from carb intake.

Once a person in on a Ketogenic diet, since they eat a fewer amount of carbs, the body can easily control the amount of blood sugar which has the capacity of reversing Type 2 diabetes.

- **Weight Loss**: What happens during ketosis? Your body shifts from burning carbs as fuel into burning fat which results in tremendous weight loss. As you dive deeper into the sea of ketosis, your body burns fat resulting in weight loss. Instead of other types of diets which may have been using for weight loss without success, with Ketogenic diet, you lose body fat and weight quickly.
- **Useful Mental Agility**: When ketosis mode is fully activated, there is a constant supply of ketones to the brain. Remember that when the body is not in ketosis mode and carb is steadily fed into the body system, the brain makes use of carb as a fuel source and many are of the opinion that to increase mental agility and focus, more carbs need to be consumed. On the contrary, when you are entirely in ketosis, your body registers a massive change in fuel consumption, meaning it burns more fat rather than the conventional carbs, resulting in fat in your body are broken down into ketone bodies. Other organs in the body can make use of fat. However, the brain makes use of ketones broken down from fat. During ketosis, there is usually an increase in the flow of ketone bodies to the brain giving it a more active mental agility and focus.

- **Acne Reduction**: It has been reported with the colossal success that many people who have acne problems when on low carb diets like the Ketogenic diet, their acne is drastically reduced. When on a Ketogenic diet the intake of carb is lowered. Where carbs are consumed, the body needs to produce the hormone called insulin to reduce the amount of blood sugar in the bloodstream. Acne is mostly caused and driven by insulin. It is the cornerstone of acne. Besides acting as the primary agent that motivate skin cells to manufacture sebum (an oily secretion secreted by the sebaceous gland for lubricating the hair and skin and protects against bacteria) and keratin (a fibrous insoluble protein that is the primary structural element in hair and nail), it heightens the secretion of many other hormones that causes acne. What does this all mean? When you are on a low carb diet like the Ketogenic diet, the flow of insulin to lower the amount of blood sugar in your bloodstream is not necessarily needed since your body does not require that. Insulin, being one of the leading causes of acne, will be curtailed since you do not consume many carbs that will summon its presence in your bloodstream. When there is no sugar to reduce in the blood, your insulin will not be used as often.
- **Enhanced Stamina**: While practicing the Ketogenic diet, your physical stamina and endurance will be improved since you will have access to storage of fat that your body has reserved.

At a time of intense exercise, your stored carbs will melt away like the dissolving ice beaten down upon by summer light. On the other hand, your fat storage can last longer than your carbs. When you are carb adapted, your fat stores are quickly depleted during a short time of intense exercise and to refill; you must keep eating. However, when you are on a Ketogenic diet, most of the fuel that is available is fat, with more long-lasting effects than your regular carb stores. Your body and your brain are energized by your fat stores making you last longer in exercise and have more stamina than someone who is relying on carbs for their strength and endurance.

- **Enhanced Performance**: Since your body is experiencing a shift from what it is used to, it is possible that at the formative stage of the Ketogenic diet you might experience some form of reduced performance. But will this remain for a long time? Certainly not. The benefits of going Ketogenic are more long term than short term. Today many athletes are going Ketogenic, and they have improved their performance, especially in long distance running. As I have explained earlier, your fat stores last longer than your carb stores. Since fat stores last longer, an athlete can perform for a prolonged period without refueling with external energy.
- **Decreased Aging**: With the Ketogenic diet, your body can and will look younger for longer. When you have entered ketosis, ketone bodies are produced.

These bodies may decrease the aging process by blocking a group of enzymes known as histone deacetylases. The enzymes function to keep a couple of genes known as Forkhead box O3 and Metallothionein 2A turned off. These genes can empower other cells to resist oxidative stress. The good thing is that the ketone bodies produce when full fledge ketosis has been entered can block Forkhead box O3 allowing the genes to be reactivated which prevents oxidative stress because it is this oxidative stress that indirectly causes aging. Besides, the Ketogenic diet reduces blood sugar levels. It is important to know that when sugar levels are reduced, glycation and the production of enhanced glycation by-product materials made from high blood sugar heightens tissue damage, diabetes, and aging. Finally, the Ketogenic diet is a catalyst that reduces triglycerides which are known for causing a lot of terminal diseases.

Alzheimer disease: This is a mental disorder that causes dementia because of the progressive degradation of the brain. One of the features of this disease is a decreasing ability to metabolize glucose. Whenever the mind is unable to metabolize glucose, it can have a lot of adverse effects on the brain. However, with ketone bodies when a person is entirely into ketosis, the supply of ketones to the brain reduces the brain's over-dependence on glucose.

Breakfast Recipes

High Protein Mascarpone Pancakes

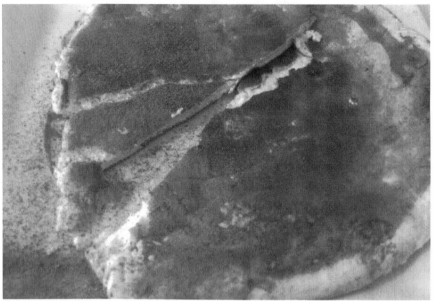

Servings: 2

Ingredients:

- 6 eggs
- 1 c. mascarpone cheese
- ¼ c. ground flax seeds
- ¼ c. chia seeds
- 1½ tsps. baking powder
- Salt

Directions:

1. Combine the flaxseed, chia seeds, baking powder and salt in a bowl. Add the eggs to the dry ingredients one at a time, whisking well after each egg.
2. Add mascarpone cheese and mix until smooth. Alternatively, place all the ingredients in a blender to achieve the same results. If you want to sweeten the batter, add about a teaspoon of sugar substitute at this point and mix well.
3. Spray cooking oil spray on a non-stick skillet and set over medium-high heat.
4. Use a large spoon or, preferably, a ladle to pour the pancake batter into the skillet once the skillet is hot.
5. Let the pancake to cook for approximately 3 minutes before carefully flipping it over with a spatula. Change to the other side and cook for about 2 minutes. Adjust the timing accordingly if you would prefer your pancakes more or less brown.
6. Serve pancakes with butter, low-carb syrup, sour cream or berries — or any combination of these options!

Nutritional Information*:* 546 Calories, 41g Fats, 12g Net Carbs, and 33g Protein.

Parmesan Eggs

Servings: 1

Ingredients:

- 2 tbsps. Parmesan cheese, fresh and grated
- 1 tbsp. whipping cream
- 1 tbsp. butter, melted
- 1 egg

Directions:

1. Preheat the oven to 350 degrees F.
2. Grease the ramekin with the butter. Dust with 1 tablespoon of the Parmesan cheese.
3. Crack the egg into the ramekin and cover with the cream. Sprinkle the remaining cheese to the mixture; bake for about 10-15 minutes, or until the egg white is set. Serve hot inside the ramekin.

Nutritional Information: 308 Calories, 27.2g Fats, 1.9g Net Carbs, and 15.8g Protein

Breakfast Squares

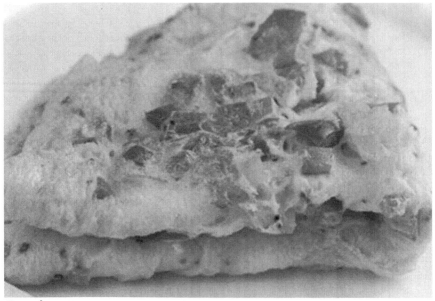

Servings: 3

Ingredients:

- 8 oz. shredded mozzarella cheese
- 8 oz. shredded cheddar cheese
- 6 large eggs
- Sliced Jalapeno peppers
- 4 tbsps. butter

Directions:
1. Carefully mix the cheeses and eggs.
2. Butter the bottom of a skillet; add the pepper and the cheese mixture; Set oven to 350F, and bake for 35 minutes, then for 30 more minutes at 250 degrees F.
3. Serve

Nutritional Information: 782 Calories, 62.6g Fats, 4.4g Net Carbs, and 51.6g Protein.

Italian Breakfast

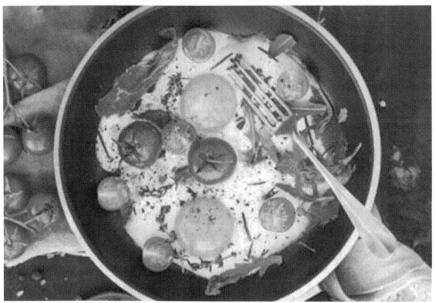

Servings: 2

Ingredients:

- 2 eggs
- 4 slices prosciutto ham
- 1 peeled clove organic garlic
- ½ c. rocket lettuce
- 10 halved cherry tomatoes
- Sea salt
- Ground black pepper
- 4 tbsps. butter

Directions:

1. Set your oven to medium-high heat. Place a tablespoon of butter in a small skillet and heat.
2. Crack and fry the eggs, preferably sunny side up, until the edges are golden (usually around 3-4 minutes). Remove from the heat and set the mixture aside for the moment.
3. Next, peel and crush the garlic clove. If need be, add more butter. Add garlic to the skillet and sauté until it begins to turn a golden brown. Add a dash of salt and pepper.
4. Sauté the halved tomatoes for about 2–3 minutes, turning halfway.
5. Optionally, saute the rocket and prosciutto for 30 seconds.
6. Everything should be ready to serve, add salt and pepper according to your taste.

Nutritional Information: 189 Calories, 3g Fats, 5g Net Carbs, and 7g Protein.

Breakfast Low Carb Mock Cinnamon

Servings: 1

Ingredients:

- ½ c. cottage cheese
- 7 toasted pecan halves
- 1 g stevia
- Cinnamon, ground
- 1½ tbsps. ghee

Directions:
1. In a large bowl, mix ghee, cottage cheese, and the sweetener.
2. Sprinkle with cinnamon and then top with the pecan halves. Serve.

Nutritional Information: 339 Calories, 28.3g Fats, 7.7g Net Carbs, and 16.6g Protein.

Apple Sausages

Servings: 6

Ingredients:

- 2 peeled, cored and diced medium sized apples
- 6 breakfast sausage links
- 4 tbsps. vegetable oil
- 1 tbsp. brown sugar

Directions:

1. Place the links in a cast-iron frying pan. Pour enough water to cover the bottom of the pan. Add the oil.
2. Set oven to medium heat and heat to evaporate water and the sausages start to change to brown.
3. Add the sweetener and apples. Cook, stirring the apple in the sausage grease until the apples are tender.

Nutritional Information*:* 162 Calories, 13.7g Fats, 9.2g Net Carbs, and 2.1g Protein.

Bacon Gravy

Servings: 4

Ingredients:

- 6 slices bacon
- 2 c. almond milk
- 2 tbsps. tapioca flour
- 2 tbsps. bacon grease
- Pepper
- Salt

Directions:

1. Set your oven to medium-high and preheat a skillet. Add bacon and cook for some time to make it crispy.
2. Remove the bacon; set aside. Drain the grease, leaving 2 tablespoons in the skillet and saving the rest for other cooking use.
3. To the skillet, add the flour and carefully whisk to combine. Take 1 minute to heat the mixture.
4. Add the milk, whisk to combine, and bring to simmer; cook for about 5-10 minutes or until the sauce starts to thicken.
5. Meanwhile, crumble the bacon. Add pepper and salt to enhance the taste. Add the bacon into the gravy. Simmer until you attain the desired consistency. Serve with biscuits.

Nutritional Information: 393 Calories, 35.5g Fats, 13.4g Net Carbs, and 8.9g Protein.

Cajun Tofu Scramble

Servings: 2

Ingredients:

- 14 ounces drained and cubed tofu
- ½ yellow onion
- 1 diced red bell pepper
- 1 diced zucchini
- 2 teaspoon Cajun seasoning
- Kale

Directions:

1. Saute onions in a skillet until transparent.
2. Add tofu and seasonings.
3. Cook for five minutes.
4. Add vegetables and cook until tender, approximately eight minutes.

Nutritional Information: 224 Calories, 12g Fats, 14g Net Carbs, and 22g Protein.

Avocado Chia Seed Pudding

Servings: 4

Ingredients:

- ¼ c. chia seeds
- 1 ripe avocado, black-skinned
- 1 c. coconut milk
- 2 medium-sized dates
- ½ teaspoon vanilla extract

Directions:
1. Blend avocado with coconut milk, dates, and spices.
2. Pour mixture over chia seeds.
3. Cover and refrigerate overnight.

Nutritional Information: 273 Calories, 24g Fats, 15g Net Carbs, and 4g Protein.

Simple Artichokes

Servings: 4

Ingredients:

- 4 big trimmed artichokes
- Salt
- Ground black pepper
- 2 tbsps. Lemon juice
- ¼ c. olive oil
- 2 tbsps. Balsamic vinegar
- 1 tsp. oregano
- 2 garlic cloves
- Water

Preparations:

1. Add water to the instant pot, add the steamer basket, add artichokes inside, cover and cook on High for 8 minutes.
2. In a bowl, mix lemon juice with vinegar, oil, salt, pepper, garlic and oregano and stir very well.
3. Cut artichokes in halves, add them to lemon and vinegar mix, toss well, place them on preheated grill with the oven set to high, cook for 3 minutes on each side, arrange them on a platter and serve as an appetizer.
4. Enjoy!

Nutritional Information: 59.3 Calories, 2.5g Fats, 8.8g Net Carbs, 2.5g Protein.

Simple Delicious Sausage Cheese Ring

Servings: 4

Ingredients:

- 2 red bell peppers
- 4 large eggs
- 1 lb. breakfast sausage
- 2 tbsps. Coconut oil
- Salt
- Ground pepper
- 4 tbsps. Shredded parmesan

Directions:

1. Add coconut oil and bell paper to instant pot cooker, set to sauté, and heat the oil.
2. Slice sausages into small rings and sauté in the hot oil for about 3 minutes. Set to the side when finished.
3. Carefully place 4 pepper rings into the instant pot. Crack an egg on a small saucer then carefully tip the plate over the pot to fill a pepper ring. Sprinkle with pepper and salt. Repeat for each ring.
4. Set sausage slices on top of eggs and cook for 10 minutes.
5. Carefully remove rings from cooker and serve with a garnish of parmesan cheese.

Nutritional Information: 470 Calories, 35.9g Fats, 3.6g Net Carbs, 28.5g Protein.

Almond Breakfast Muffins

Servings: 4

Ingredients:

- 1¼ c. almond flour
- ½ tsp. sea salt
- ½ tsp. baking soda
- 3 large eggs
- ¼ c. almond slivers
- 3 tbsps. coconut oil
- 1 tbsp. coconut flakes
- 6 bacon strips
- 1 c. grated parmesan cheese
- 2 tsps. Stevia
- 1 tsp. vanilla

Directions:

1. In a mixing bowl, pre-sift the blanched almond flour to obtain the desired consistency. Add eggs and then vanilla; give about 30 strokes with a large spoon and add almond slivers, coconut flakes, stevia and 2 tablespoons of coconut oil.
2. In a coconut oil greased cupcake pan, scoop about two tablespoons of batter and bake at 350 degrees F for about 15 minutes.
3. Garnish with crumbled bacon just as they come out of the stove.

Nutritional Information: 82 Calories, 7.2g Fats, 3.1g Net Carbs, 2.1g Protein.

Power Berry Vanilla Keto Pancakes

Servings: 3

Ingredients:

- 4 egg yolks
- 1½ c. cottage cheese
- 1 tbsp. unbleached flour
- 1 tbsp. almond flour
- 2 tbsps. Coconut oil
- 1 tsp. vanilla extract
- 1 c. blackberries
- ¼ c. raspberries
- 1 c. heavy whipping cream
- 1 tsp. Stevia

Directions:
1. Mix all the above-stated ingredients in a mixing bowl. Do not over mix.
2. Cook on a hot skillet using coconut oil until it bubbles on the sides and flip.
3. Cook until golden brown.
4. Mix topping together and top.

Nutritional Information: 388 Calories, 34.9g Fats, 2.7g Net Carbs, 16.7g Protein.

Eggs and Chives

Servings: 3

Ingredients:

- 3 tbsps. Ghee
- 3 tbsps. Cream cheese
- 3 large eggs
- 1 tbsp. chopped chives
- Salt
- Black pepper
- 1 c. water

Directions:

1. Divide grease 3 ramekins with the ghee and divide cream cheese in each.
2. In each ramekin, crack an egg, season with salt and black pepper and sprinkle chives on top.
3. Add water to the instant pot, add the steamer basket, add ramekins inside, cover and cook on High for 2 minutes.
4. Serve hot.
5. Enjoy!

Nutritional Information: 163 Calories, 4g Fats, 7g Net Carbs, 6g Protein.

Eggs and Cheese Breakfast

Servings: 4

Ingredients:

- 2 c. riced cauliflower
- 6 chopped bacon slices
- 6 large eggs
- ¼ c. coconut milk
- ½ c. shredded cheddar cheese
- Salt
- Black pepper
- 1 small chopped yellow onion
- 1½ c. water

Directions:

1. Set your instant pot on sauté mode, add bacon, stir and cook for 2 minutes.
2. Add the onion, stir and cook for 2 minutes more.
3. Add cauliflower rice, stir and cook for 2 minutes.
4. In a bowl, mix eggs with cheese, salt, pepper, coconut milk and the veggie mix, stir everything and pour into a heatproof dish.
5. Clean your instant pot, add the water and the trivet, add the baking dish inside, cover and cook on High for 10 minutes.
6. Divide between plates and serve. Enjoy!

Nutritional Information*: 82 Calories, 3g Fats, 7g Net Carbs, 7g Protein.

Decadent High Fat Pancakes

Servings: 5

Ingredients:

For Syrup:
- 2 tbsps. Maple syrup
- ½ c. Sukrin fiber syrup

For Pancakes:
- 4 eggs, large
- 2 tbsps. erythritol
- ½ tsp. baking soda
- ¾ c. nut butter of your choice
- 1/3 c. coconut milk
- 2 tbsps. ghee
- 1 tsp. cinnamon

Directions:

1. Add maple syrup and Sukrin fiber syrup into a jar or small bowl and use a spoon to stir until combined. Cover and put the jar or small bowl aside until needed.
2. Put eggs, erythritol, baking soda, coconut milk, nut butter and cinnamon powder in a food processor and pulse until blended.
3. Heat ghee in a non-stick skillet and use about a ¼ cup per pancake. Cook until pancake sets then flip and finish cooking; place on a plate.
4. Repeat with remaining batter and plate.
5. Top with syrup and serve.

Nutritional Information: 401 Calories, 32.5g Fats, 3.6g Net Carbs, 12.8g Protein.

Breakfast Bacon and Avocado Muffins

Servings: 16

Ingredients:

- ½ c. almond flour
- 1½ tbsps. psyllium husk powder
- 4 oz. Colby jack cheese
- 1 tsp. baking powder
- 1 tsp. garlic
- 1 tsp. chives
- 3 spring onions
- 1 tsp. dried cilantro
- ¼ tsp. red chili flakes
- Salt
- Pepper
- 1½ tbsps. lemon juice
- 5 eggs
- ¼ c. flaxseed meal
- 1½ c. coconut milk
- 5 bacon slices
- 2 cubed avocados
- 2 tbsps. butter

Directions:

1. Add flour, spices, lemon juice, eggs, flaxseed meal and coconut milk to a bowl. Mix together until thoroughly combined.
2. Heat a skillet and cook bacon strips until crispy then add the butter and avocado.
3. Add the bacon and avocado mixture to batter and mix together.
4. Set oven to 350 F and grease cupcake molds.
5. Add batter to molds and bake for 26 minutes. Take from oven and cool before removing from mold.
6. Serve. Store leftovers in the fridge.

Nutritional Information: 163 Calories, 14.1g Fats, 1.5g Net Carbs, 6.1g Protein.

Zesty Cinnamon Scones

Servings: 8

Ingredients:

- ¼ c. erythritol
- ¼ tsp. stevia
- 1 tbsp. flax seeds
- ½ tsp. baking powder
- 1 orange
- 1½ tsps. cinnamon
- ½ tsp. sea salt
- 8 tbsps. coconut flour
- ¼ c. butter

- 2 large eggs
- 2 tbsps. maple syrup
- ½ tsp. xanthan gum
- 1/3 c. heavy cream
- 1½ tsp. vanilla extract

Icing:

- 20 drops stevia
- 1 tbsp. orange juice
- ¼ c. coconut butter

Directions:

1. Set oven to 400 degrees Fahrenheit.
2. Place dry ingredients in a large bowl except for xanthan and 1 tbsp coconut flour. Add butter to dry mix and stir to combine.
3. Combine sweetener and eggs until thoroughly mixed and light in color. Put in maple syrup, remaining flour, xanthan gum, heavy cream and vanilla; mix until combined and thick.
4. Add wet mixture to dry, reserving 2 tbsp of liquids, mix together and add cinnamon and use hands to form mixture into dough. Shape into a ball and press into a cake like a shape. Slice into 8 pieces.
5. Place onto a lined baking sheet and use reserved liquid to brush the top of scones.
6. Bake for 15 minutes, remove from oven and cool.
7. Prepare icing and drizzle over scones before serving.

Nutritional Information: 232 Calories, 20g Fats, 3.3g Net Carbs, 3.3g Protein.

Mozzarella, Bacon and Pepper Frittata

Servings: 6

Ingredients:

- 1 tbsp. olive oil
- 7 bacon sliced
- 1 chopped red bell pepper
- ¼ c. heavy cream
- ¼ c. parmesan cheese
- 9 eggs
- Salt
- Pepper
- 2 tbsps. chopped parsley
- 4 c. Bella mushrooms
- ½ c. chopped basil
- 4 oz. cubed mozzarella cheese
- 2 oz. chopped goat cheese

Directions:

1. Set oven to 350 F.
2. In a frying pan heat, olive oil over high heat then add bacon and cook for 5 minutes until browned.
3. Add red pepper and cook for 2 minutes until soft. While pepper cooks, add cream, parmesan cheese, eggs, parsley, salt, and pepper to a bowl and whisk to combine.
4. Add mushrooms to pot, stir and cook for 5 minutes until soaked in fat. Add basil, cook for 1 minute and then add mozzarella.
5. Add in the egg mixture and use a spoon to move ingredients around so that the egg reaches the bottom of the pan.
6. Top with goat cheese and place in oven for 8 minutes then broil for 6 minutes.
7. Use a knife to pry frittata edges from pan and slice.

Nutritional Information: 408 Calories, 31.2g Fats, 2.4g Net Carbs, 19.2g Protein.

Cheese and Sausage Pies

Servings: 2

Ingredients:

- 1½ pieces chicken sausage
- ½ tsp. rosemary
- ¼ tsp. baking soda
- ¼ c. coconut flour
- ¼ tsp. chili flakes
- 1 tsp. salt
- 5 egg yolks
- 2 tsp. lemon juice
- ¼ c. coconut oil
- 2 tbsps. coconut milk
- ¾ grated cheddar cheese

Directions:

1. Set oven to 350 F.
2. Chop sausage, heat skillet and cook sausage. While sausages cook, combine dry ingredients in a bowl. In another bowl combine egg yolks, lemon juice, oil and coconut milk. Add liquids to dry mixture and add ½ cup of cheese; fold to combine and put into 2 ramekins.
3. Add cooked sausages to the batter and use a spoon to push into the mixture.
4. Bake for 25 minutes until golden on top. Top with leftover cheese and broil for 4 minutes.
5. Serve warm.

Nutritional Information: 711 Calories, 65.3g Fats, 5.8g Net Carbs, 34.3g Protein.

Lunch Recipes

Garlicky Chicken Livers

Servings: 1

Ingredients:

- ½ lb. chicken liver
- 1 tsp. lemon juice
- 2 tbsps. olive oil
- 2 tbsps. melted ghee
- 3 cloves garlic
- Salt

Directions:
1. Wash the chicken livers. Trim and dry them.
2. Dry-fry them in a nonstick frying pan for about 4 minutes without the use of oil.
3. To the pan, add lemon juice, ghee-olive oil, and salt to taste. Stir once to mix.
4. Sprinkle the garlic and serve.

Nutritional Information: 858 Calories, 68.3g Fats, 5.1g Net Carbs, and 56.1g Protein.

Chicken Bacon Wraps

Servings: 12

Ingredients:

- 12 skinless and boneless chicken breast halves
- 12 slices of bacon
- 16 oz. chive and onion cream cheese
- 12 tbsps. divided olive oil spread
- Salt

Directions:

1. Flatten the chicken breasts to 1/2-inch thickness.
2. Spread 3 tablespoons of cream cheese over each chicken breast.
3. Dot with 1 tablespoon olive oil spread and sprinkle with the salt; roll up and wrap each rolled piece with a bacon strip.
4. Grease your pan and place chicken onto it and bake uncovered for about 40 minutes at 400 degrees F or until the juices run clear.
5. Transfer the pan 6 inches from the heat source; broil for 5 minutes until the bacon is crispy.

Nutritional Information: Calories 502, Total Fat 38.2 g, Protein 38.1 g, Total Carbs 1.1 g

Cauliflower Salad

Servings: 4

Ingredients:

Salad:

- 1 head cauliflower, medium
- 1½ c. mushrooms, sliced
- 1½ tbsps. olive oil
- 1 tsp. fresh dill
- 1 tsp. chives, chopped
- ½ tsp. paprika, smoked
- Salt

- Pepper

Sauce:

- ½ c. extra-virgin olive oil
- ¼ c. soy milk, unsweetened
- 1 tsp. cider vinegar, raw
- Salt
- White pepper

Directions:

1. Make the salad; cut cauliflower into tiny florets.
2. Place the cauliflower florets into a pan and cover with water.
3. Bring to a boil and reduce heat. Simmer for 3-4 minutes or until crisp-tender.
4. In the meantime, heat olive oil in a skillet. Cook mushrooms for 5-8 minutes or until soft. Toss in the cauliflower and shake to coat with oil. Season to taste with salt and pepper.
5. Make the sauce; make sure oil and milk are equal temperatures. It is a significant step.
6. Place soy milk, cider vinegar, and seasonings in a food blender. Blend until smooth. While the blender is running low, gradually stream in extra-virgin olive oil.
7. Blend until thickens.
8. In a bowl, toss cauliflower with prepared sauce, dill, and chives.
9. Divide between bowls and sprinkle with paprika. Chill briefly before serving.

Nutritional Information*:* Calories 588, Total Fat 49 g, Protein 19 g, Total Carbs 19 g

Salt-and-Pepper Stir-Fried Shrimp

Servings: 6

Ingredients:

- 4 cloves garlic, chopped
- 2 tsps. divided salt
- 2 tbsps. vegetable
- 2 lbs. shrimp
- ½ tsp. Red peppercorn
- ½ tsp. white peppercorn
- ½ tsp. black peppercorn
- ½ tsp. green peppercorn
- 1 c. chopped cilantro leaves

Directions:

1. Crush the peppercorns in a mortar.
2. Into a large bowl, place the shrimp, salt and half of the crushed peppercorns; toss to coat the shrimp evenly and set aside.
3. Heat a large nonstick pan over high heat. Add the garlic, oil, and the remaining peppercorns and salt; cook for about 1 minute, continually stirring, until fragrant.
4. Add the shrimp to the mixture and cook for about 4 minutes as you stir.
5. Add the cilantro; turn off the heat; and toss to combine.
6. Serve right away.

Nutritional Information: Calories 335, Total Fat 10.6 g, Total Carbs 4.8 g, Protein 52 g

Almond Buns

Servings: 6

Ingredients:

- 2 eggs
- ¾ c. almond flour
- 5 tbsps. Butter, unsalted
- 1½ tsp. baking powder
- 1½ tsp. stevia or Splenda

Directions:

1. Combine the dry ingredients in a bowl.
2. Whisk in the eggs.
3. Melt butter and add it to the mixture.
4. Divide the mixture into equal 6 parts; place into a muffin top pan or something similar
5. Bake at 350 degrees F for about 12-17 minutes. You may need to watch the first time you make these since cooking time will vary depending on your oven.
6. Let cool on a wire rack.

Nutritional Information: Calories 184, Total Fat 17.2 g, Protein 4.7 g, Total Carbs 4.3 g

Stuffed Portabella with Nut Pate

Servings: 4

Ingredients:

- 4 portabella mushrooms caps
- 1 tbsp. olive oil
- 1 tbsp. coconut aminos
- Pepper
- Salt

Nut pate:

- 1 c. soaked macadamia nuts
- 1 tbsp. coconut aminos
- 1 chopped celery stalk
- Kosher salt

Directions:

1. Heat oven to 375F and line a baking sheet with parchment paper.
2. In a bowl, beat olive oil with coconut aminos. Brush in mushroom caps with oil mixture and arrange onto a baking sheet.
3. Bake for 15 minutes.
4. In the meantime, make the nut paste; rinse and drain macadamia nuts. Place the macadamia nuts and celery in a food processor and process until just smooth. In the last seconds of processing, add coconut aminos and salt to taste.
5. Process until the coconut aminos is incorporated.
6. Remove the portabella from the oven and place on a plate. Fill with macadamia pate and serve warm.

Nutritional Information: Calories 158, Total Fat 9.4 g, Protein 10 g, Total Carbs 12.7 g

7.

Creamy Cauliflower Soup

Servings: 4

Ingredients:

- 2 c. cauliflower florets
- 2 c. wild mushrooms, sliced
- 2 c. coconut milk, full-fat
- 2 tbsps. avocado oil
- 1 tsp. celery flakes, dried
- ½ tbsps. Thyme, freshly chopped
- 1 minced clove garlic
- Salt
- Pepper

Directions:

1. In a saucepan, mix celery flakes, cauliflower, and coconut milk.
2. Cover and bring to a boil over medium-high heat.
3. Reduce heat and simmer for 6-7 minutes. Kill the heat and puree using an immersion blender.
4. In the meantime, heat avocado oil in a skillet. Add thyme and garlic. Cook until fragrant. Toss in wild mushrooms and cook for 6-7 minutes or until tender.
5. Pour in pureed cauliflower and bring to a boil. Reduce heat and simmer 6-8 minutes or until thickened.
6. Serve warm with Keto bread.

Nutritional Information: Calories 240, Total Fat 1 g, Protein 10 g, Total Carbs 50 g

Spicy Garlic Butter Shrimp

Servings: 5

Ingredients:

- 4 lbs. large-sized shrimp, unpeeled
- 2 tbsps. garlic, minced
- ½ c. butter
- Lemon pepper seasoning
- Garlic powder

Directions:

1. Preheat the oven to 300 degrees F.
2. Mix the butter and the garlic.
3. Place the shrimp in a saucepan and dot with the garlic butter; sprinkle well with the garlic powder and the lemon pepper.
4. In an open state, bake for about 30 minutes, stirring once or twice, until the shrimp are opaque, making sure the shrimp is evenly cooked.
5. Serve alongside the butter sauce that is in a separate bowl or the one containing the shrimp for dipping.
6. You may serve alongside cauliflower rice.

Nutritional Information: 749 Calories, 30.7g Fats, 8.3g Net Carbs, and 103.8 g Protein.

Sticky Drumsticks

Servings: 8

Ingredients:

- 8 chicken drumsticks
- ½ c. olive oil
- ¼ c. sweet chili sauce
- 2 garlic cloves, minced
- ¼ c. soy sauce
- 2 tsps. sesame seeds

Directions:

1. Slice through the thickest part of each drumstick using a sharp knife. Arrange them in a glass dish.
2. In a bowl, mix the sauces and garlic. Rub all over the drumstick; marinate for about 30 minutes in the refrigerator.
3. Preheat the oven to 248 degrees F of 356 for the fan.
4. Place the drumsticks on a nonstick baking paper. Sprinkle them with sesame seeds. Bake for about 45 minutes. Let cool slightly; serve.

Nutritional Information: 209 Calories, 16.7g Fats, 1.2g Net Carbs, and 13.4g Protein.

Grilled Spicy Lime Shrimp

Servings: 8

Ingredients:

- 1 lb. peeled and deveined medium shrimp
- 1 juiced lime
- ½ c. vegetable oil
- 3 tbsps. Cajun seasoning

Directions:

1. In a Ziploc bag, mix the Cajun seasoning, lime juice, and vegetable oil. Add the shrimp, shake to coat, squeeze out the excess air, seal the bag, and marinate for 20 minutes in the refrigerator.
2. Preheat an outdoor grill to medium heat. Lightly grease the grate.
3. Take the shrimp from marinade as you shake off any excess; discard marinade.
4. Allow cooking both sides for 2 minutes each. Serve.

Nutritional Information: 188 Calories, 3g Fats, 1.2g Net Carbs, and 13g Protein.

Instant Pot Olive Steamed Fish

Servings: 4

Ingredients:

- 4 white fish fillets
- 1 c. pitted and chopped olives
- 1 lb. halved cherry tomatoes
- ½ tsp. dried thyme
- 1 minced garlic clove
- Olive oil
- Salt
- Black pepper
- 1 c. water

Directions:
1. Put the water in your instant pot.
2. Put fish fillets in the steamer basket of the pot.
3. Add tomatoes and olives on top.
4. Also add garlic, thyme, oil, salt, and pepper.
5. Cook on Low for 10 minutes while the pot is covered.
6. Release the pressure, uncover the pot, divide fish, olives and tomatoes mix among plates and serve. Enjoy!

Nutritional Information: 157 Calories, 3.3g Fats, 0g Net Carbs, 29g Protein.

Coconut Milk Beef Curry

Servings: 4

Ingredients:

- 2 lbs. cubed beef steak
- 2 tbsps. Extra virgin olive oil
- 3 diced potatoes
- 1 tbsp. wine mustard
- 2½ tbsps. Curry powder
- 2 chopped yellow onions
- 2 minced garlic cloves
- 10 oz. canned coconut milk
- 2 tbsps. Tomato sauce
- Salt
- Black pepper

Directions:

1. Set your instant pot on Sauté mode, add the oil and heat it up.
2. Add onions and garlic, stir and cook for 4 minutes.
3. Add potatoes and mustard, stir and cook for 1 minute.
4. Add beef, stir and brown on all sides. Add curry powder, salt, and pepper, stir and cook for 2 minutes.
5. Add coconut milk and tomato sauce, stir, cover the pot and cook at High for 10 minutes. Release the pressure, uncover the pot, divide curry among plates and serve.

Nutritional Information: 434 Calories, 20g Fats, 14g Net Carbs, 27.5g Protein.

Ginger Short Ribs

Servings: 4

Ingredients:

- 2 chopped green onions
- 1 tsp. vegetable oil
- 3 minced garlic cloves
- 3 slices of ginger
- 4 lbs. short ribs
- ½ c. water
- ½ c. soy sauce
- ¼ c. rice wine
- ¼ c. pear juice
- 2 tsps. Sesame oil

Directions:

1. Set your instant pot on Sauté mode, add the oil and heat it up.
2. Add green onions, ginger and garlic, stir and cook for 1 minute.
3. Add ribs, water, wine, soy sauce, sesame oil and pear juice, stir and cook for 2-3 minutes.
4. Cover the pot and cook at High for 45 minutes.
5. Release the pressure naturally for 15 minutes, uncover the pot and transfer the ribs to a plate.
6. Strain liquid from the pot, divide ribs among plates and drizzle the sauce all over.

Nutritional Information: 300 Calories, 11g Fats, 5g Net Carbs, 10g Protein.

Steak and Salsa

Servings: 3

Ingredients:

- 1 diced beef tomatoes
- 1 tbsp. olive oil
- ½ diced red onion
- ½ bunch chopped cilantro
- Salt
- Pepper
- 1 lb. sliced stewing beef
- 1 sliced bell pepper

- ½ sliced onion
- 4 tbsps. Butter
- 2 tbsps. Mixed dry seasoning:
- 1 tsp. cumin
- ½ tsp. sweet paprika
- ½ tsp. paprika flakes
- 1 tsp. garlic salt
- ½ tsp. black pepper

Directions:

1. Cover bottom of crock-pot with the salsa.

2. Add remaining ingredients and mix well.

3. Cover, cook on low for 6-8 hours.

Nutritional Information: 40 Calories, 22g Fats, 6g Net Carbs, 38g Protein.

Chili Beef Stew

Servings: 6

Ingredients:

- 3 lbs. stewing beef
- 2 cans Italian tomatoes
- 1 c. beef broth
- 4 tbsps. Butter
- 1 tsp. Cayenne pepper
- 1 tbsp. Worcestershire sauce
- 1 tsp. oregano, dried
- 1 tsp. thyme, dried
- Salt
- Pepper

Directions:

1. Add all the ingredients to the crock-pot, mix well.

2. Cover, cook on high for 6 hours.

3. Break up the beef with a fork, pull apart in the crock-pot.

4. Taste and adjust the seasoning, if needed.

5. Re-cover, cook for an additional 2 hours on low.

Nutritional Information: 295 Calories, 25g Fats, 10g Net Carbs, 62g Protein.

☐

Dinner Recipes

Chicken Cacciatore with Spaghetti Squash

Servings: 6

Ingredients:

- 4 skinless chicken thighs
- 1 medium diced Onion
- 1 bell peppers
- 2 minced cloves Garlic
- ½ tsp. thyme, dried
- 1 c. Chicken stock
- 28 oz. tomatoes, diced
- 8 oz. Tomato sauce
- ½ tsp. dried basil
- Salt
- Pepper
- ½ diced yellow squash
- ½ tsp. dried oregano
- 1 Spaghetti squash

Directions:

1. Dice the veggies. Set them aside.
2. Cut the chicken up. Season it as desired.
3. Place the chicken in a Dutch oven and let it brown for about 8 minutes.
4. Add in the onion, garlic and bell pepper and let them cook for approximately 5 minutes or until the onions soften.
5. Add the chicken tomato sauce, tomatoes, and the chicken stock.
6. Season as desired and mix well before letting everything boil.
7. Turn the heat to low and let everything cook for 30 minutes.
8. Add the yellow squash. Cook between 15 and 30 more minutes.

Nutritional Information: Calories 267, Total Fats 5.1g, Protein 40g, Total Carbs 17g

Meat-Based Pizza

Servings: 1

Ingredients:
- Small package of Ground uncooked beef
- Salsa
- 1 diced Onion
- Italian Spices
- Garlic powder
- Shredded Mozzarella cheese
- 6 strips Bacon

Directions:

1. Dice onion and put the onion into a baking dish.
2. Add the beef, salsa, garlic powder and other spices into a baking dish. Mix together.
3. Shred the cheese and put it evenly over the top of the beef mixture.
4. Cut the bacon into small pieces and put the pieces on top of the cheese.
5. Ensure your oven is set to 375 degrees F
6. Place the pizza in the oven and let it cook for 35 minutes.

Nutritional Information: Calories 195, Fats 24g, Protein 17g, Net Carbs 1.2g

Mexican Casserole

Servings: 12

Ingredients:

- ½ tsp. Cumin
- 1 head Cauliflower
- ½ white Onion
- ½ tsp. Chili powder
- 1 Green bell pepper
- 1½ c. Parmesan
- 1 hashed Bell pepper
- 4 chopped Cherry tomatoes

Directions:

1. Ensure your oven is set to 350 degrees Fahrenheit.
2. Place the skillet on top of the stove over a burner set to medium heat.
3. Roast the chili powder, pepper, cumin, and onion, stirring regularly until the veggies are fully cooked.
4. Dice the cauliflower. Cook it in the microwave for 3 minutes.
5. Put the tomatoes and 1 cup of the cheese in with the cauliflower. Mix.
6. Mix the results with the vegetables.
7. Using cooking spray coat a baking dish.
8. Add the vegetable mixture to the baking dish.
9. Add the rest of the cheese.
10. Place the dish in the oven and let it cook for approximately 40 minutes.
11. Garnish as desired.

Nutritional information: Calories 69, Total Fats 30g, Protein 3.56g, Total Carbs 4.5g

Tasty Fried Chicken Breast

Servings: 1

Ingredients:

- 1 Chicken breast
- Butter
- Salt
- Pepper
- Curry powder
- Garlic powder
- ½ c. Greens

Directions:

1. Cut chicken into small chunks.
2. Heat up the butter in a frying pan.
3. Put the chicken into the pan. Stir to coat chicken.
4. Add spices to taste.
5. Stir-fry until the chicken browns and gets crunchy.
6. Serve with greens on the side.

Nutritional Information: Calories 189, Total Carbs 1g, Protein 27g, Total Fat 8g

Baby-Back Ribs

Servings: 4

Ingredients:

- 4 lbs. baby back pork ribs
- 2 tbsps. sugar
- 2 tbsps. chili powder
- ½ tsp. mustard powder
- ½ tsp. thyme leaves, dried
- Salt

Directions:

1. Preheat the oven to 300F or light an outdoor grill.
2. In a small bowl, except for the ribs, combine the rest of the ingredients; rub the mixture on each side of the ribs.
3. If using a grill, cook the ribs with the bone-side down over medium-low heat or when the coals are covered with ash. Adjust the flame and add coals if necessary; cook for about 1½ hours.
4. If using an oven, place the ribs with the bone-side down; cook for 1½ hours.
5. The ribs are cooked when the ribs separate when you insert a fork between them.

Nutritional Information: 1252 Calories, 81.1g Fats, 3.8g Net Carbs, and 120.7g Protein.

Almond-Crusted Tilapia

Servings: 4

Ingredients:
- 4 (each 6 oz.) tilapia fillets
- 2 tbsps. olive oil
- 2 tbsps. butter
- ¼ c. tapioca flour
- Salt
- 1 c. sliced almonds, divided

Directions:

1. Place ½ cup of the almonds in the food processor until chopped into beautiful pieces. Transfer into a shallow bowl. Add the flour, mix until combined.
2. Evenly sprinkle the fillets with salt and dredge with the almond-flour mixture.
3. In a large skillet, melt the butter with the olive oil over medium heat. Add the fish; cook for about 4 minutes per side or until golden brown. Transfer the fillets into a serving plate.
4. Add the remaining almond into the skillet; cook for 1 minute, frequently stirring, or until golden.
5. With a slotted spoon, remove the almonds; sprinkle over the fillets.

Nutritional Information: 415 Calories, 26.2g Fats, 11.5g Net Carbs, 36.7g Protein.

Perfect Boneless Pork Tenderloin

Servings: 4

Ingredients:

- 1 lb. pork tenderloin, boneless
- Onion powder
- Any of the following or a mixture (rosemary, thyme, garlic powder, or savory)
- Salt
- Pepper

Directions:

1. Determine the exact weight of your roast from the meat wrapper. This will determine how long you need to cook it.
2. Preheat the oven to 500F.
3. Season the meat according to your preference. Place uncovered on a shelf in the bottom 1/3 of the oven.
4. Bake EXACTLY for 5½ minutes PER POUND. Adjust the time according to your oven's heat retention and accuracy.
5. Turn the oven off. Do not open the door for about 45 minutes to 1 hour. If your oven has a probe thermometer, you can open the oven door when it alerts that the temperature is 140F.
6. Remove the pork from the oven; cover lightly with foil; and let rest for about 5 -10 minutes to redistribute the internal juices.

Nutritional Information: 162 Calories, 4g Fats, 0g Net Carbs, and 29.7g Protein.

Basil Tomato Salmon

Servings: 2

Ingredients:

- 2 boneless salmon fillets
- 4 tbsps. olive oil
- 1 thinly sliced tomato
- 1 tbsp. basil, dried
- 2 tbsps. Parmesan cheese, grated

Directions:
1. Preheat the oven to 375F.
2. Take an aluminum foil and line the baking sheet and grease it with nonstick cooking spray.
3. Place the salmon on the foil; sprinkle with the basil; top with the tomato; drizzle with the olive oil, or sprinkle with parmesan.
4. Bake for about 20 minutes, or until the salmon center is opaque and the cheese is lightly browned on top.

Nutritional Information: 374 Calories, 41.6g Fats, 1.8g Net Carbs, 37.9g Protein.

Cheesy Tuna Casserole

Servings: 4

Ingredients:

- 12 oz. drained Tuna
- 16 oz. frozen Green beans
- 3 oz. sliced fresh mushrooms
- 2 tbsps. Butter
- ½ c. Chicken broth
- ¾ c. Heavy cream
- 2 chopped Onions
- Salt
- Pepper
- Xanthan gum
- 1 stalk hashed Celery
- 8 oz. shredded Cheddar cheese

Directions:

1. Cook the green beans in a medium pot. Drain well.
2. Place the butter, celery, mushrooms, and onion in a pan and place the pan on top of the stove over a burner turned to medium heat and let everything cook for 5 minutes.
3. Add the broth. Boil, letting the liquid cook down by half.
4. Stir in the cream. Let come back up to a boil.
5. Turn down the heat until the sauce is thickened, stirring frequently. Don't let it boil over.
6. Season to taste.
7. Put the mushroom and tuna mixture into the green beans.
8. Add salt and pepper if needed.
9. Put the cheese in it, thoroughly mixing it in.
10. Put the mixture into a 1.5 or 2-quart casserole dish.
11. Microwave or bake until hot.

Nutritional Information*:* 459 Calories, 33g Fats, 12g Net Carbs, 31g Protein.

Ground Beef and Bell Peppers

Servings: 2

Ingredients:

- 1 diced Onion
- Coconut oil
- 1 lb. beef, ground
- 1 c. freshly chopped Spinach
- Salt
- Pepper
- 1 sliced red Bell pepper

Directions:
1. Chop the spinach. Set aside.
2. Dice the onion into tiny pieces.
3. Add the oil to a skillet before placing the skillet on the stove over a burner set to medium heat. Add in the onion and coat well in oil. Let it cook for 60 seconds.
4. Mix in the spinach and the beef and stir well. Season as desired.
5. Stir-fry everything until cooked.
6. Put the sliced fresh bell pepper on a serving plate, and dish up the cooked meat mixture beside the peppers.

Nutritional Information: 380 Calories, 22g Fats, 6.2g Net Carbs, and 25g Protein.

Meat Bacon Tacos

Servings: 3

Ingredients:

- 1 lb. cooked hamburger
- ½ c. taco sauce
- ¼ c. ranch dressing
- 2 c. shredded lettuce, thinly sliced
- ½ c. tomatoes, diced
- 20 strips bacon
- 2 whisked eggs

Directions:

1. On a plastic microwave bacon dish, lay out 5 strips of bacon over the cooking mold to form a "taco shell." Brush with egg wash and microwave until it forms a shell, about 4 minutes.
2. Cook hamburger meat and add ¼ cup taco sauce.
3. Now add all the ingredients to build a taco. This includes dividing all ingredients into the 4 tacos you will make.
4. If you do not want all the bacon, you can substitute small torts.
5. Another possibility is to create a taco bowl out of this by adding the lettuce and diced bacon with all the rest of the ingredients in a small bowl.
6. Finally, add a dash of tobacco sauce for a bite.

Nutritional Information: 300 Calories, 21g Fats, 15g Net Carbs, 12g Protein.

Zucchini & Almond Pesto

Servings: 2

Ingredients:

- 2 cubed medium Zucchinis
- 1 cubed avocado
- ¼ c. walnuts
- ¼ c. basil leaves, fresh
- ¼ c. almond slices
- 2 peeled cloves garlic
- ½ juiced lemon
- ¼ c. Parmesan cheese, grated
- 1 tbsp. olive oil
- ½ tbsp. Italian seasoning
- Salt
- Pepper

Directions:
1. This recipe is easy to make. In your food processor, place all the above ingredients and grind until a smooth paste, about 30-45 seconds.
2. The pesto can be eaten cold like a dip.
3. You can add the pesto to other recipes for flavor and food enhancement. For example baked chicken with the pesto on top.

Nutritional Information: 130 Calories, 9g Fats, 9g Net Carbs, 6g Protein.

☐

Salmon and Veggies

Servings: 4

Ingredients:

- 4 boneless salmon fillets
- 2 c. water
- 3 tbsps. Olive oil
- 1 sliced lemon
- 1 chopped white onion,
- 3 sliced tomatoes
- 4 chopped thyme sprigs
- 4 chopped parsley sprigs
- Salt
- Black pepper

Directions:

1. Drizzle the oil on a parchment paper.
2. Add a layer of tomatoes, salt, and pepper.
3. Drizzle some oil again, add fish and season with salt and pepper.
4. Drizzle some more oil, add thyme and parsley, onions, lemon slices, salt and pepper and wrap packet.
5. Add water to the instant pot, add the steamer basket, add packet inside, cover and cook on High for 15 minutes.
6. Unwrap packet, divide fish and veggies between plates and serve.
7. Enjoy!

Nutritional Information: 200 Calories, 5g Fats, 10g Net Carbs, 20g Protein.

Shrimp and Turnips

Servings: 4

Ingredients:

- 2 lbs. deveined shrimp
- 1 lb. chopped tomatoes
- 1 c. water
- 3 quartered turnips
- 4 tbsps. olive oil
- 4 chopped onions
- 1 tsp. ground coriander
- 1 tsp. curry powder
- Juice of 1 lemon
- Salt
- Black pepper

Directions:

1. Put the water in your instant pot, add steamer basket, add turnips, cover pot, cook on High for 6 minutes, drain, transfer to a bowl and leave aside for now.
2. Clean your instant pot, set it on sauté mode, add oil, heat it up, add onions, stir and cook for 5 minutes.
3. Add salt, coriander, curry, tomatoes, lemon juice, shrimp, and turnips, stir, cover and cook on High for 6 minutes more.
4. Divide shrimp into bowls and serve.
5. Enjoy!

Nutritional Information: 183 Calories, 4g Fats, 7g Net Carbs, 15g Protein.

Spaghetti & Meat Squash

Servings: 2

Ingredients:

- 2 Spaghetti squash
- 2 tbsps. coconut oil
- 1 lb. ground beef, grass fed
- 1 c. Parmesan cheese
- 1 tsp. chili powder
- 1 tsp. Italian seasoning
- ½ tsp. oregano
- 2 minced cloves garlic
- 3 c. spaghetti sauce
- ¼ c. coconut flour

Directions:

1. Set your oven to 350 degrees F and cook spaghetti squash for an hour. Cut the squash into long strips. Add to mixing bowl with coconut flour and coconut oil and gently fold with a spatula until thoroughly mixed.
2. Next, cook beef with all the spices until brown. Do NOT drain fat and add spaghetti sauce.
3. Finally place spaghetti squash on the plate first, add parmesan cheese (divide among servings).
4. Now add spaghetti sauce with meat on top and serve immediately.
5. You can add pepper flakes or chili spice for more zest.

Nutritional Information: 341 Calories, 12g Fats, 17g Net Carbs, 24g Protein.

Lebanese Chicken Thighs

Servings: 4

Ingredients:

- 4 chicken thighs
- 2 c. water
- 1 chicken bouillon cube
- ¼ c. garlic olive oil
- 2 tbsps. Butter
- 1 quartered white onion
- 2 diced carrots
- 2 diced celery stalks
- 2 small quartered tomatoes
- 1 juice of a lemon
- ¼ c. soy sauce
- 3 c. diced lettuce and field greens

Directions:
1. Set oven to high. Mix all ingredients using a mixing bowl and pour over chicken.
2. Cook for 30 minutes while the bowl is covered.
3. On a plate put 2 thighs on about 2 cups of the greens and scoop a cup of the broth from the chicken and pour over it.
4. One variant is to add parmesan cheese over the greens.
5. Another variant is to add ½ a cup of olives.
6. Serve immediately.

Nutritional Information: 107 Calories, 5g Fats, 0g Net Carbs, 14g Protein.

Snacks

Brown-Butter Roasted Pecans with Rosemary

Servings: 4

Ingredients:

- 4 c. pecan halves
- 2 tsps. sugar
- 2 tsps. kosher salt
- ¼ c. butter
- 1 tbsp. fresh rosemary, chopped
- Rosemary leaves, fresh

Directions:
1. Preheat the oven to 350F.
2. In a medium-sized saucepan; cook the butter over medium heat for about 3-5 minutes constantly stirring, until it starts to turn golden brown. Remove immediately from the heat; stir in the pecans. Arrange the butter coated pecans in a single layer on a baking sheet; sprinkle with the salt and sugar.
3. Bake pecans for about approximately 12 minutes, or until fragrant and toasted, stirring halfway through baking; sprinkle with the rosemary. Bake for another 2 minutes; let cool completely on the baking sheet, about 30 minutes.
4. Store in airtight container if there are any leftovers.

Nutritional Information: 645 Calories, 66.6g Fats, 12.7g Net Carbs, and 9.2g Protein.

Cheesy Chili Dip

Servings: 8

Ingredients:

- 10 oz. Kraft Old English cheese
- 4 oz. cream cheese
- ½ c. sour cream
- ¼ c. freshly chopped cilantro
- 2 tbsps. minced canned chipotle chili in adobo sauce

Directions:

1. In a food processor, blend the English cheese, cream cheese, sour cream, and chipotle until the mixture is soft. Stir in the cilantro, cover, and chill for at least 2 hours before serving.
2. Serve with assorted sliced vegetables or low carb chips or crackers.

Nutritional Information: 364 Calories, 31.9g Fats, 3.1g Net Carbs, and 16.9g Protein.

Bacon-Jalapeno Poppers

Servings: 12

Ingredients:

- 25 jalapeno peppers, fresh
- 2 c. shredded cheddar cheese
- 16 oz. cream cheese
- 32 oz. chopped bacon

Directions:

1. Cut the stems of the jalapeño peppers and then cut them lengthwise; remove the seeds.
2. Fill each with the cream cheese; sprinkle the top with the cheddar cheese; and wrap each cheese-stuffed jalapeño with bacon.
3. Place on baking sheets, and bake for about 10-15 minutes in a 450F preheated oven, or until the bacon is cooked thoroughly.
4. Kill the heat and allow to cool; and serve.

Nutritional Information: 755 Calories, 61.7g Fats, 5.4g Net Carbs, and 43.2g Protein.

Oven-Fried Coconut Chicken Drumsticks

Servings: 4

Ingredients:

- 2 large eggs
- 12 chicken drumsticks
- 1 c. coconut flour
- 1 c. shredded coconut, unsweetened
- 2 tbsps. coconut oil

Directions:

1. The first step is to preheat the oven to about 400 degrees Celsius
2. In a bowl, whisk the two eggs lightly
3. Mix the shredded coconut and the coconut flour in a bowl.
4. Each of the 12 drumsticks is dipped in the whisked egg then finally in the coconut mixture.
5. Place a pan in the oven to slightly heat before melting the 2 tablespoons of the coconut oil.
6. Fry each drumstick for about 2 minutes before placing them on a wire rack.
7. In an oven, place the wire rack containing the drumsticks for a minimum of 40 minutes
8. After the 40 minutes, it is advisable to let the drumstick rest for a maximum of 10 minutes. This will allow the juices in the meat to settle.

Nutritional Information: 256 Calories, 8.6g Fats, 15.6g Net Carbs, and 27.7g Protein.

Three Cheese Bacon Tomato Frittata

Servings: 8

Ingredients:

- 6 slices bacon
- 1 c. cherry tomatoes
- 10 large eggs
- ¼ c. heavy cream
- ¼ c. parmesan cheese
- ¼ c. feta cheese crumbles
- ½ c. sharp cheddar cheese, shredded

Directions:

1. First, it is important for you to slice the bacon to bite size. Fry the pieces over medium heat while on a pan. This is let until the bacon is crunchy.
2. Once the bacon has become crispy, add the sliced cherry tomatoes then cook for about 4 minutes.
3. Whisk all the 10 eggs in a large bowl. Add the ¼-cup cream into the bowl then mix them appropriately.
4. Include the cheese in the bowl containing the whisked eggs-cream mixture. Use a spatula to make a homogeneous mixture.
5. The ultimate egg mixture is poured into a pan then allowed to cook for like 2 minutes.
6. Into an oven with a temperature of about 375 degrees Celsius, place the pan containing the egg mixture for about 25 minutes.
7. The meal is ready to serve 8 dishes.

Nutritional Information: 210 Calories, 16.3g Fats, 2.9g Net Carbs, and 13.8g Protein.

Sea Salt Cheese Crackers Gluten Free

Servings: 6

Ingredients:

- 1 c. almond flour
- 1 egg
- ¼ c. golden flax seed meal
- ½ tsp. baking soda
- Salt
- 1 c. sharp cheddar cheese

Directions:

1. In a food processor, add the almond flour, salt, baking soda, flax seed, and cheese. Turn on the processor to ensure the ingredients combine homogeneously.
2. To the uniform mixture, add oil and egg to form a ball.
3. Onto the cookie sheet, press the formed balls to make a dough
4. Sprinkle the salt over the dough. Using your hands spread the salt evenly over the whole area.
5. Use a pizza cutter to cut the flat almond mixture into smaller shapes of your choice.
6. Preheat the oven to about 350F for about 15 minutes.
7. While still hot, retrace the shapes you cut earlier using a pizza cutter.
8. Allow 10 minutes to cool the meal before enjoying the service.
9. Preheat outdoor grill on medium-high temperature, light oil the grate

Nutritional Information: 130 Calories, 3g Fats, 22g Net Carbs, and 2g Protein.

Avocado Slices

Servings: 2

Ingredients:

- 2 ripe avocados
- ¼ c. coconut cream, whipped
- 1 c. almond meal
- 1 c. olive oil
- 1 cayenne pepper
- Salt

Chili dip:

- 1 c. extra-virgin olive oil
- ½ c. almond milk
- 2 tsps. cider vinegar
- 1 tsp. chili powder
- Salt

Directions:
1. Peel, pit, and slice avocados.
2. Place whipped coconut cream in a small bowl.
3. In a separate bowl, combine almond meal with salt and cayenne pepper.
4. Heat oil in a deep pan.
5. Place avocado pieces into the heated oil and fry 45 seconds.
6. Transfer to a paper-lined plate.
7. Make a chili dip; blend all dip ingredients, except the oil in a food blender until smooth. Stream in oil and blend until creamy. Serve with avocado slices.

Nutritional Information: 50 Calories, 5g Fats, 3g Net Carbs, and 1g Protein.

Chili Dip

Servings: 8

Ingredients:

- 5 dried and chopped ancho chilies
- 2 minced garlic cloves
- Salt
- Black pepper
- 1½ c. water
- 2 tbsps. balsamic vinegar
- 1½ tsps. stevia
- 1 tbsp. chopped oregano
- ½ tsp. ground cumin

Directions:

1. In your instant pot mix water chilies, garlic, salt, pepper, stevia, cumin and oregano, stir, cover and cook on High for 8 minutes.
2. Blend using an immersion blender, add vinegar, stir, set the pot on simmer mode and cook your chili dip until it thickens.
3. Serve with veggie sticks on the side as a snack.
4. Enjoy!

Nutritional Information: 85 Calories, 1g Fats, 2g Net Carbs, 2g Protein.

Artichoke Dip

Servings: 6

Ingredients:

- 14 oz. artichoke hearts
- 8 oz. cream cheese
- 8 oz. shredded mozzarella cheese
- 16 oz. grated parmesan cheese
- 10 oz. spinach
- 1 tsp. onion powder
- ½ c. chicken stock
- ½ c. coconut cream
- 3 minced garlic cloves
- ½ c. mayonnaise

Directions:

1. In your instant pot, mix artichokes with stock, garlic, spinach, cream cheese, coconut cream, onion powder and mayo, stir, cover and cook on High for 5 minutes.
2. Add mozzarella and parmesan, stir well, transfer to a bowl and serve as a snack.
3. Enjoy!

Nutritional Information: 200 Calories, 3g Fats, 4g Net Carbs, 7g Protein.☐

Desserts and Smoothies

Peanut Butter Mousse

Servings: 4

Ingredients:
- ½ can coconut cream
- 4 tbsps. peanut butter, unsweetened
- 1 tsp. stevia

Directions:

1. Combine all ingredients and whip for one minute, until mixture forms peaks.
2. Chill for at least three hours, or until a mousse texture is achieved.

Nutritional Information: 206 Calories, 18g Fats, 6g Net Carbs, and 5g Protein.

Almond butter balls

Servings: 14

Ingredients:

- 3 tbsps. almond butter
- 3 tbsps. carob powder
- 3 tsps. almond flour
- 2 tsps. powdered Yacon powder
- ½ c. coconut flakes, unsweetened

Directions:

1. In a bowl, combine almond butter, carob powder, almond flour, and Erythritol.
2. Stir until combined.
3. Place coconut flakes in a small bowl.
4. Scoop prepared a mixture with a small ice cream scoop and drop into coconut flakes.
5. Roll until completely covered with the coconut flakes. Arrange the balls on a plate and refrigerate for 4-6 hour or until firm.
6. Serve and enjoy.

Nutritional Information: 135 Calories, 9g Fats, 18g Net Carbs, and 4g Protein.

Peanut Butter Cookies

Servings: 12

Ingredients:

- 1 c. smooth peanut butter
- ¾ c. almond flour
- ½ c. powdered Erythritol
- ¼ c. almond milk
- 1 scoop hemp protein powder, vanilla flavored
- 1 tsp. baking soda

Directions:

1. Heat oven to 350F and line a baking sheet with baking paper.
2. In a bowl, cream peanut butter, and powdered Erythritol.
3. In a separate bowl, combine all dry ingredients.
4. Fold the dry ingredients into peanut butter and stir until you have a crumbly mix.
5. Stir in almond milk and roll dough into balls (2 tablespoons per cookie).
6. Drop dough onto baking sheet and flatten with a fork, making a crisscross pattern.
7. Bake cookies 10 minutes. Cool completely before serving.

Nutritional Information: 135 Calories, 7g Fats, 17g Net Carbs, and 2.6g Protein.

Stuffed Apples

Servings: 4

Ingredients:

- 4 cored green apple
- ½ c. melted coconut butter
- ¼ c. almond butter, unsweetened
- 2 tbsps. Cinnamon, ground
- Ground nutmeg
- Salt
- 4 tbsps. Shredded and unsweetened coconut
- 1 c. water

Directions:

1. In a bowl, mix together coconut butter, almond butter, cinnamon, nutmeg, and salt.
2. Arrange the apples in a slow cooker and place the water in the bottom. With a spoon, place butter mixture into each apple evenly. Top each apple with shredded coconut.
3. Set the slow cooker on Low. Cover and cook for about 2-3 hours.
4. Serve warm.

Nutritional Information: 352 Calories, 25.7g Fats, 34.5g Net Carbs, and 1.4g Protein.

Berry Crumble

Servings: 6

Ingredients:

- 1 c. almond flour
- 2 tbsps. melted butter
- 1 tbsp. applesauce, unsweetened
- 4 c. fresh mixed berries
- 1 tbsp. chopped butter

Directions:

1. In a bowl, add flour, melted butter, and applesauce and mix until crumbly mixture forms.
2. In the bottom of a slow cooker, place the berries and dot with chopped butter. Sprinkle the topping mixture over the berries evenly.
3. Set the slow cooker on Low. Cover and cook for about 2 hours.
4. Unplug the slow cooker and let the crumble cool slightly. Cut into desired pieces and serve warm.

Nutritional Information: 142 Calories, 10g Fats, 11.7g Net Carbs, and 1.9g Protein.

Cocoa Pumpkin Fudge

Servings: 24

Ingredients:
- 1 c. organic unsweetened pumpkin puree
- 1¾ c. cocoa butter
- 1 tsp. allspice
- 1 tbsp. coconut oil, melted

Directions:

1. Line 8-inch glass dish with baking paper.
2. Melt cocoa butter over medium heat.
3. Stir in pumpkin puree and allspice. Stir to combine.
4. Add coconut oil and stir well. Transfer the mixture into a prepared glass dish and press down to distribute evenly.
5. Cover with a second piece of baking paper and refrigerate 2 hours.
6. Slice and serve.

Nutritional Information: 91.1 Calories, 7.2g Fats, 8.5g Net Carbs, and 0.5g Protein.

Blackberry cheesecake smoothie

Servings: 1

Ingredients:

- 6 Ice cubes
- Sweetener
- ¾ c. Coconut milk
- ¼ tsp. Vanilla extract
- 1 tsp. Coconut oil
- ¼ c. frozen blackberries
- ¼ c. Water

Directions:

1. Cream the coconut milk: This is a simple process. All you need to do is place the can of coconut milk in the refrigerator overnight. The next morning, open the can and spoon out the coconut milk that has solidified. Don't shake the can before opening. Discard the liquids.
2. Add all of the ingredients, save the ice cubes, to the blender and blend on low speed until pureed. Thin with water as needed.
3. Add in the ice cubes and blend until the smoothie reaches your desired consistency.

Nutritional Information: 515 calories, 6.7g net carbs, 53g fats, 6.4g protein

Orangesicle smoothie

Servings: 1

Ingredients:

- 6 Ice cubes
- Sweetener
- ¾ c. Coconut milk
- 1 scoop Vanilla whey protein
- 2 tbsps. Coconut oil
- 2 oz. Plain skyr
- 8 oz. Fresh orange juice
- 2 oz. shredded Carrot
- 1 ripe Mango

Directions:

1. Cream the coconut milk: This is a simple process. All you need to do is place the can of coconut milk in the refrigerator overnight. The next morning, open the can and spoon out the coconut milk that has solidified. Don't shake the can before opening. Discard the liquids.

2. Add all of the ingredients, save the ice cubes, to the blender and blend on low speed until pureed. Thin with water as needed.

3. Add in the ice cubes and blend until the smoothie reaches your desired consistency.

Nutritional Information: 328 calories, 7g net carbs, 12g fats, 8g protein

Vanilla ice cream smoothie

Servings: 1

Ingredients:

- 6 Ice cubes
- Sweetener
- ¼ c. Mascarpone
- 2 Egg yolk
- 1 tbsp. Coconut oil
- ¼ tsp. Vanilla extract
- 1 oz. Whipped topping

Directions:
1. Add all of the ingredients, save the ice cubes, to the blender and blend on low speed until pureed. Thin with water as needed.
2. Add in the ice cubes and blend until the smoothie reaches your desired consistency.
3. Top with whipped topping prior to serving.

Nutritional Information: 651 calories, 4g net carbs, 64g fats, 12g protein

Strawberry rhubarb pie smoothie

Servings: 1

Ingredients:

- 6 Ice cubes
- Sweetener
- ¾ c. Coconut milk
- 5 tsps. Powdered Ginger
- ¼ tsp. Vanilla extract
- 2 tbsps. Almond butter
- 2 Rhubarb stalks
- 1.4 oz. Strawberries
- 1 Organic egg
- ¼ tsp. Vanilla extract
- 5 grated Ginger root

Directions:

1. Cream the coconut milk: This is a simple process. All you need to do is place the can of coconut milk in the refrigerator overnight. The next morning, open the can and spoon out the coconut milk that has solidified. Don't shake the can before opening. Discard the liquids.
2. Add all of the ingredients, save the ice cubes, to the blender and blend on low speed until pureed. Thin with water as needed.
3. Add in the ice cubes and blend until the smoothie reaches your desired consistency.

Nutritional Information: 392 calories, 6.6g net carbs, 31g fats, 14.2g protein

Avocado Pudding

Servings: 4

Ingredients:
- 2 pitted and chopped avocados
- 2 tsps. vanilla extract
- 8 drops stevia
- 1 tbsp. lime juice
- 14 oz. coconut milk
- 1½ c. water

Directions:

1. In your instant pot, mix avocado with coconut milk, vanilla extract, stevia and lime juice, blend well and divide into 4 ramekins.
2. Add the water to your instant pot, add the steamer basket, add ramekins inside, cover and cook on High for 2 minutes.
3. Keep puddings in the fridge until you serve them.
4. Enjoy!

Nutritional Information: 150 calories, 3g net carbs, 3g fats, 4g protein

Orange Cake

Servings: 12

Ingredients:

- 6 large eggs
- 1 quartered orange
- 1½ c. water
- 1 tsp. vanilla extract
- 1 tsp. baking powder
- 9 oz. almond meal
- 4 tbsps. swerve
- 2 tbsps. grated orange zest
- 2 oz. stevia
- 4 oz. cream cheese
- 4 oz. coconut yogurt

Directions:

1. In your food processor, mix orange with almond meal, swerve, eggs, baking powder, and vanilla extract, pulse well and transfer to a cake pan.
2. Add the water to your instant pot, add steamer basket, add cake pan inside, cover and cook on High for 25 minutes.
3. In a bowl, mix cream cheese with orange zest, coconut yogurt, and stevia and stir well.
4. Spread this well over cake, slice and serve it.
5. Enjoy!

Nutritional Information: 170 calories, 4g net carbs, 3g fats, 4g protein

Icy Pops

Servings: 6

Ingredients:

- 1 peeled and pitted avocado
- 1½ tsps. vanilla paste
- 1 c. coconut milk
- 2 tbsps. almond butter
- Drops of stevia
- ¼ tsp. Ceylon cinnamon

Directions:
1. Combine all ingredients in a food blender.
2. Blend until smooth.
3. Transfer the mixture into popsicle molds and insert popsicle sticks.
4. Freeze 4 hours or until firm.
5. Serve.

Nutritional Information: 41 Calories, 0.1g Fats, 10g Net Carbs, and 0g Protein.

Spicy Mango Dip

Servings: 4

Ingredients:

- 1 chopped shallot
- 1 tbsp. coconut oil
- ¼ tsp. cardamom powder
- 2 tbsps. minced ginger
- ½ tsp. cinnamon powder
- 2 chopped mangos
- 2 chopped red hot chilies
- 1 chopped apple
- ¼ c. raisins
- 5 tbsps. stevia
- 1¼ apple cider vinegar

Directions:

1. Set your instant pot on Sauté mode, add oil, heat it up, add shallot and ginger, stir and cook for 3 minutes.
2. Add cinnamon, hot peppers, cardamom, mangos, apple, raisins, stevia, and cider, stir, cover and cook on High for 7 minutes.
3. Set the pot on simmer mode, cook your dip for 6 minutes more, transfer to bowls and serve cold as a snack.
4. Enjoy!

Nutritional Information: 100 Calories, 2g Fats, 3g Net Carbs, 1g Protein.

Cranberry Dip

Servings: 4

Ingredients:

- 2½ tsps. grated lemon zest
- 3 tbsps. lemon juice
- 12 oz. cranberries
- 4 tbsps. stevia

Directions:

1. In your instant pot, mix lemon juice with stevia, lemon zest, and cranberries, stir, cover and cook on High for 2 minutes.
2. Set the pot on simmer mode, stir your dip for a couple more minutes, transfer to a bowl and serve with some biscuits as a snack.
3. Enjoy!

Nutritional Information: 73 Calories, 0g Fats, 2g Net Carbs, 2g Protein.

Conclusion

I do hope that this book has been helpful and you found the information contained within the chapters useful!

For those who have already been able to make the mental conversion to change, then I trust, that you will find this a far more accessible and easy to maintain eating method than those you may have tackled in the past. I am convinced that just a few weeks on the Ketogenic diet will produce such good results that you will be encouraged to turn it into a permanent way of life.

Keep in mind that you are not only limited to the recipes provided in this book! Just go ahead and keep on exploring until you create your very own culinary masterpiece!

Stay healthy and stay safe!

Peter Bragg

14154818R00096

Made in the USA
Lexington, KY
05 November 2018